IT'S TIME TO EAT NANCE FRUIT

It's Time to Eat
NANCE FRUIT

Walter the Educator

Silent King Books
A WhichHead Entertainment Imprint

Copyright © 2024 by Walter the Educator

All rights reserved. No part of this book may be reproduced in any manner whatsoever without written per- mission except in the case of brief quotations embodied in critical articles and reviews.

First Printing, 2024

Disclaimer

This book is a literary work; the story is not about specific persons, locations, situations, and/or circumstances unless mentioned in a historical context. Any resemblance to real persons, locations, situations, and/or circumstances is coincidental. This book is for entertainment and informational purposes only. The author and publisher offer this information without warranties expressed or implied. No matter the grounds, neither the author nor the publisher will be accountable for any losses, injuries, or other damages caused by the reader's use of this book. The use of this book acknowledges an understanding and acceptance of this disclaimer.

It's Time to Eat NANCE FRUIT is a collectible early learning book by Walter the Educator suitable for all ages belonging to Walter the Educator's Time to Eat Book Series. Collect more books at WaltertheEducator.com

USE THE EXTRA SPACE TO TAKE NOTES AND DOCUMENT YOUR MEMORIES

NANCE FRUIT

The sun is shining, skies are blue,

It's Time to Eat
Nance Fruit

Guess what time it is, I'll give you a clue!

Tiny and golden, round and neat,

It's time to eat some nance fruit sweet!

Nance fruit grows where it's warm and bright,

In tropical lands, a sunny delight.

They dangle in bunches, high on a tree,

Yellow and juicy, just for me!

Pick them fresh or buy them near,

The smell of nance is oh so clear.

It's sweet and tangy, such a treat,

A little fruit that can't be beat!

Some like it raw, just one by one,

Popping nance is so much fun.

Others blend it into a drink,

A splash of flavor, what do you think?

It's Time to Eat
Nance Fruit

In syrup, nance is sticky and sweet,

A dessert that's perfect to eat.

With ice cream or cake, it tastes divine,

A fruity treat for any time.

Grandma says, "Try it in stew,

Nance adds a flavor that's special and new."

In sauces or soups, it's such a surprise,

This little fruit is truly wise.

Nance is small but packed with cheer,

A bite of sunshine any time of year.

Golden yellow, sometimes red,

It makes my tummy happy and fed.

"Let's share!" I say, "with family and friends,

The joy of nance never ends."

We pass the bowl, take a bite,

It's Time to Eat
Nance Fruit

Laughing together feels so right.

"Save the seeds," my sister says,

"We'll plant a tree in sunny rays!"

Someday soon, it'll grow so tall,

With golden nance for us all.

So when it's nance time, don't delay,

Enjoy this fruit in every way.

Sweet and tangy, yellow and bright,

It's Time to Eat
Nance Fruit

Nance fruit makes the world feel right!

ABOUT THE CREATOR

Walter the Educator is one of the pseudonyms for Walter Anderson. Formally educated in Chemistry, Business, and Education, he is an educator, an author, a diverse entrepreneur, and he is the son of a disabled war veteran. "Walter the Educator" shares his time between educating and creating. He holds interests and owns several creative projects that entertain, enlighten, enhance, and educate, hoping to inspire and motivate you. Follow, find new works, and stay up to date with Walter the Educator™ at WaltertheEducator.com